# Sam and Little Bear

Story by Beverley Randell

Illustrations by Pat Reynolds

Mom said,

"Go to bed, Sam."

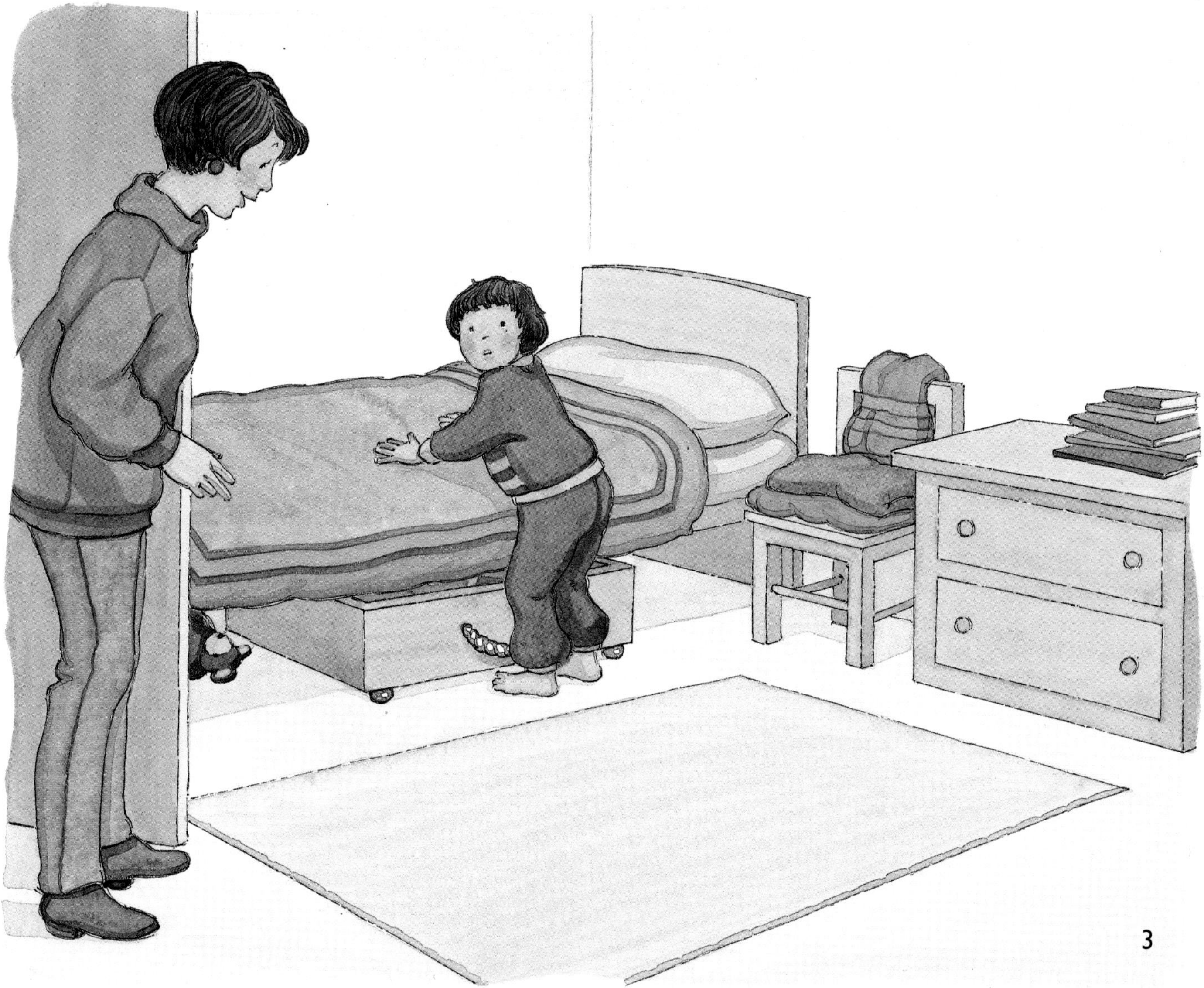

"I can not go to bed,"
said Sam.
"Little Bear is not in bed.
Where is he?"

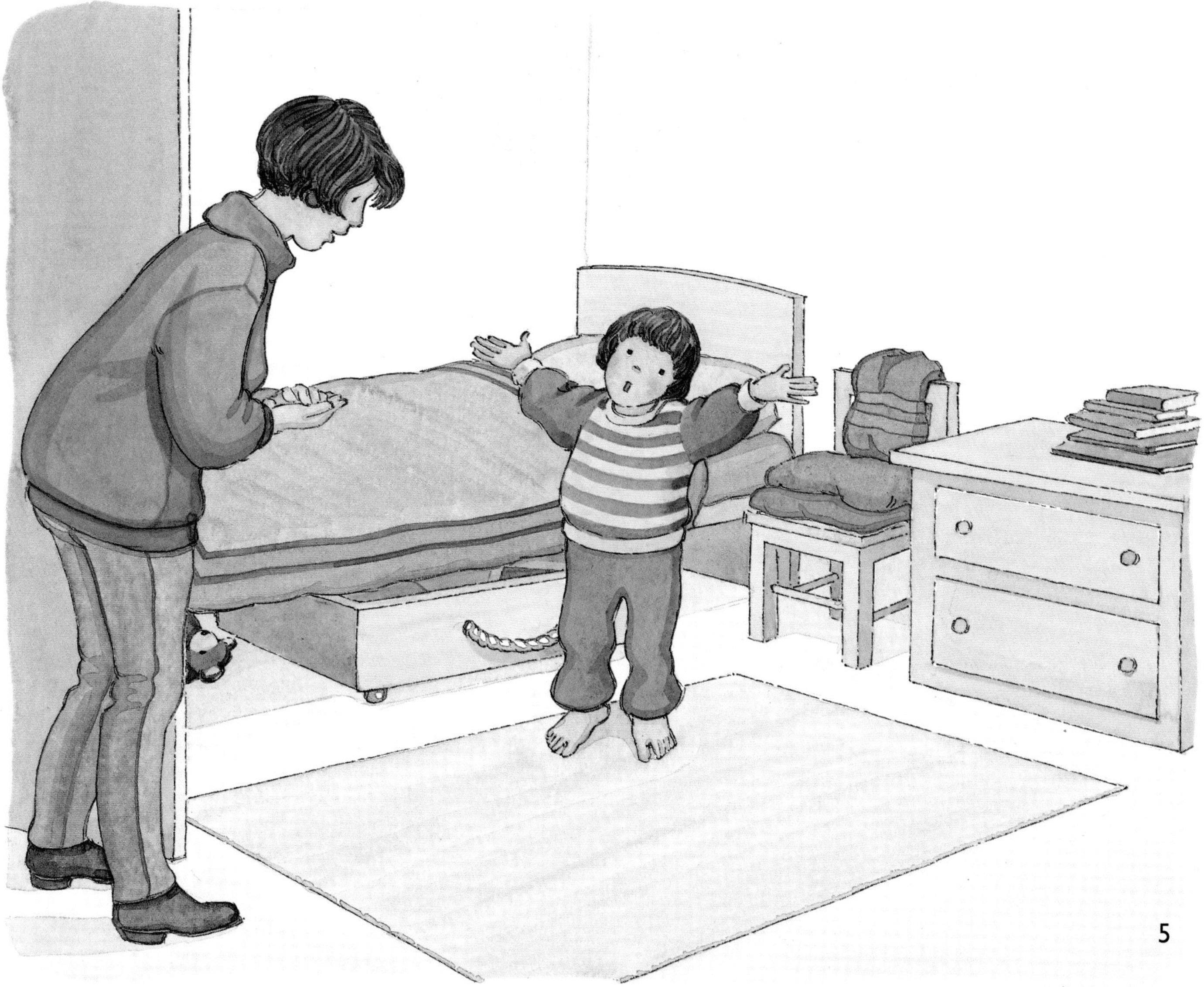

Sam looked and looked
for Little Bear.

Mom looked and looked
for Little Bear, too.

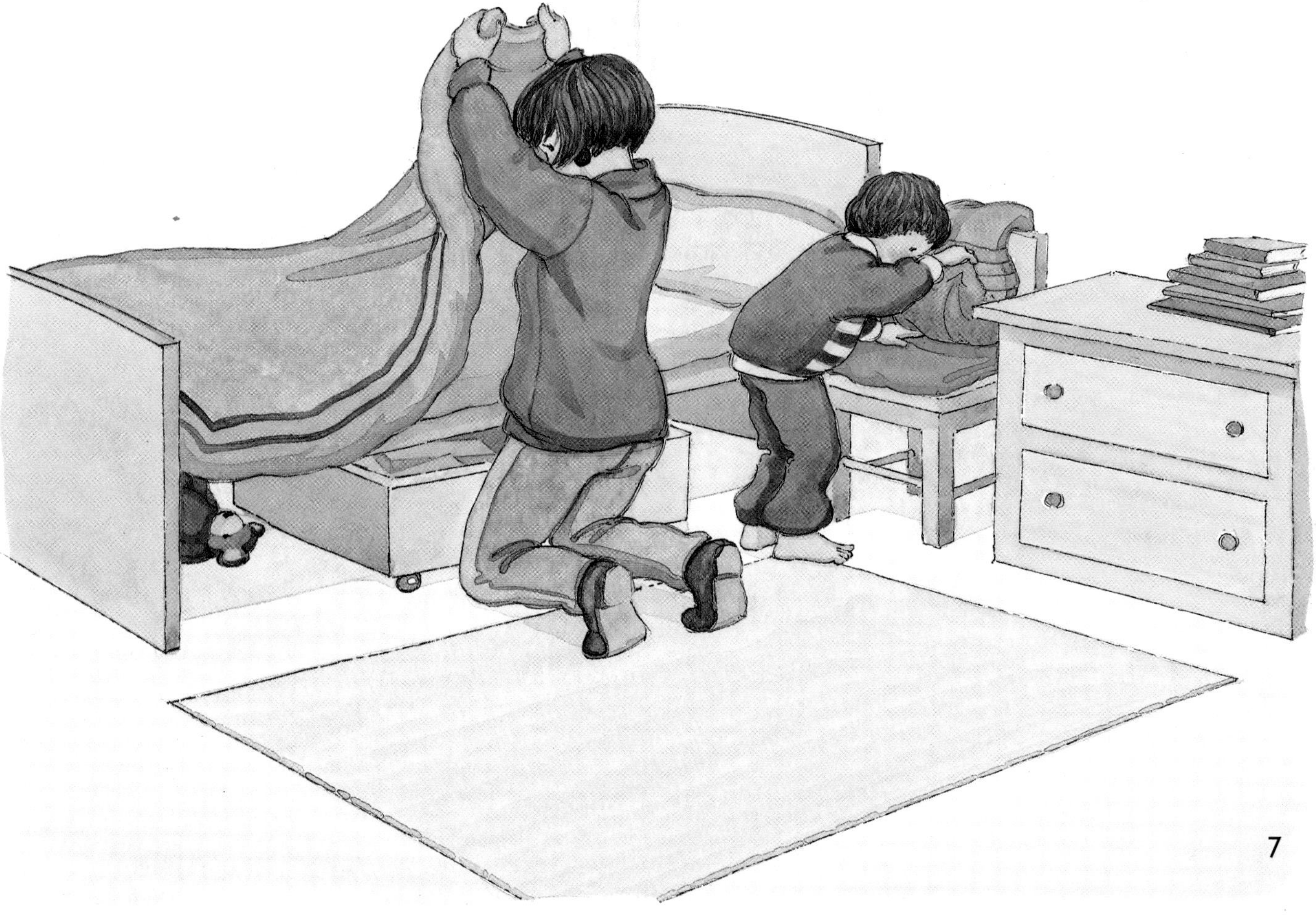

"Where is Little Bear?"
said Sam.
"Where **is** he?"

"He is not in here,"
said Mom.

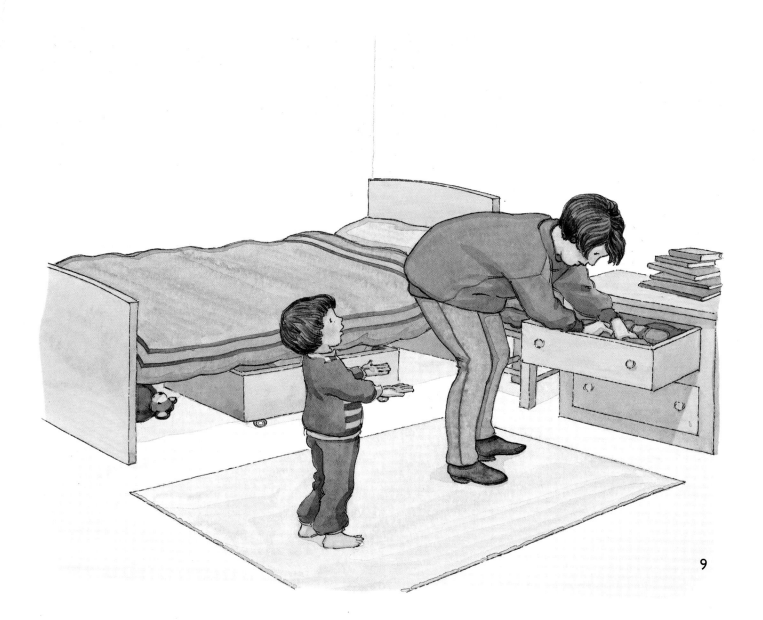

Sam and Mom

looked in the box.

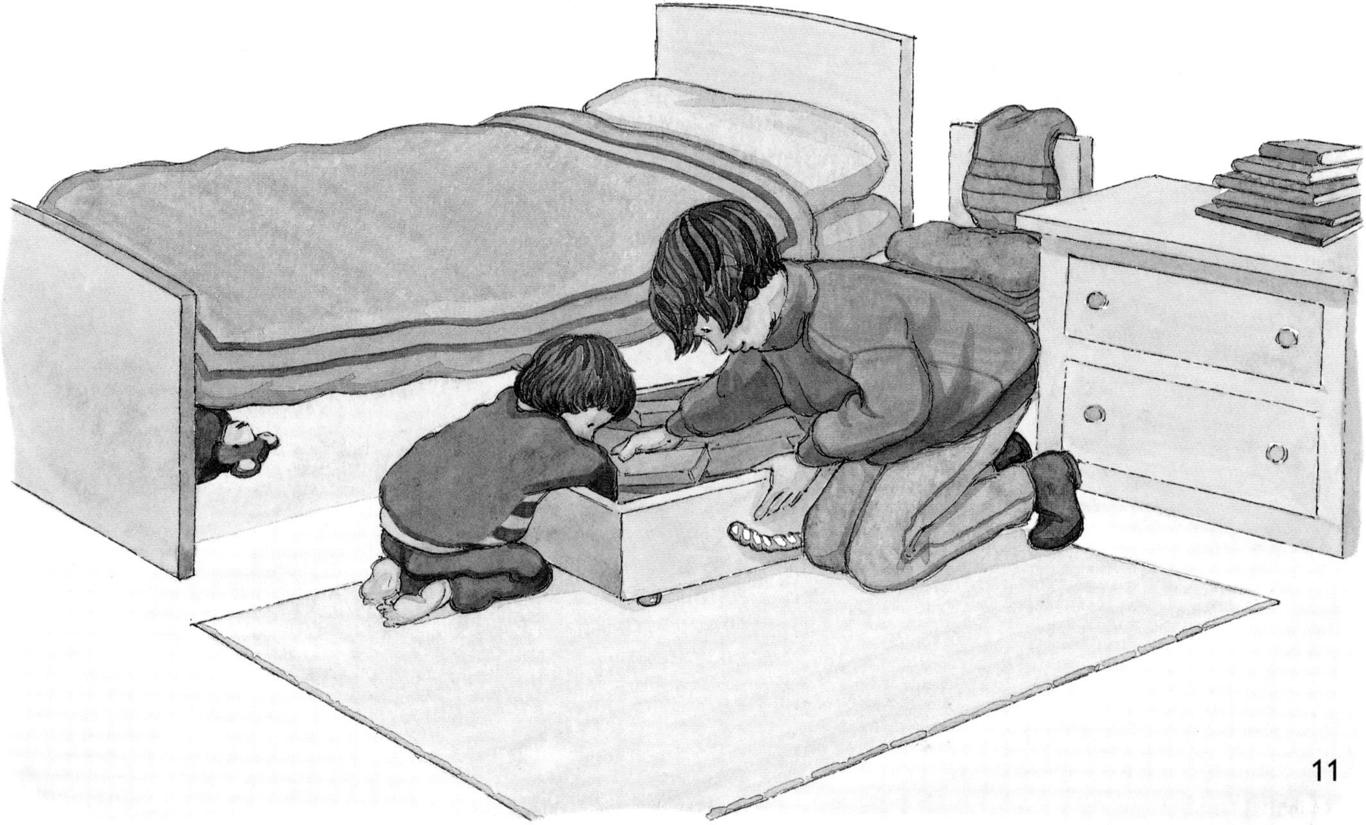

"Little Bear is not

in the box," said Sam.

"Look, Mom!

Here he is!"

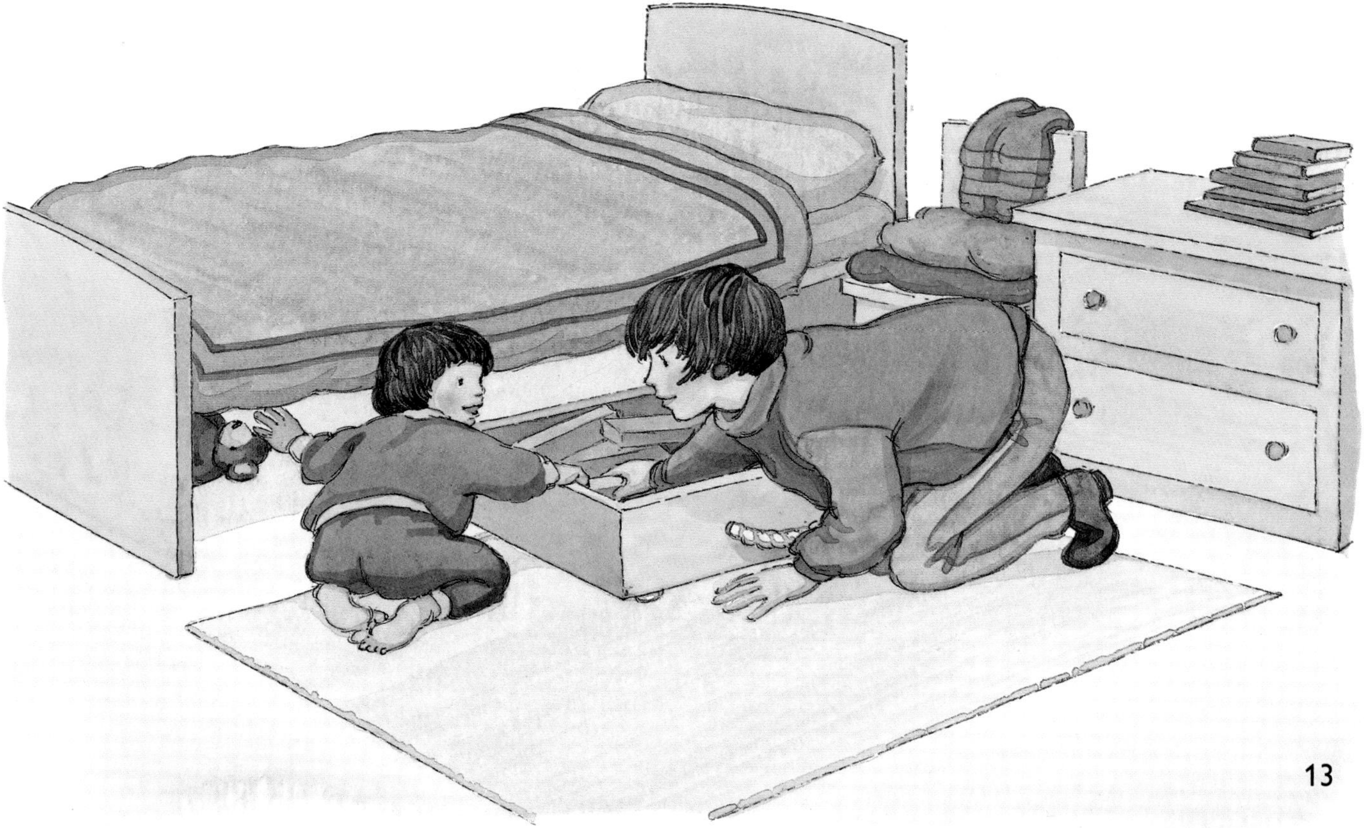

"Go to bed, Little Bear,"
said Mom.

"Come on, Little Bear,"
said Sam.

"Come to bed."

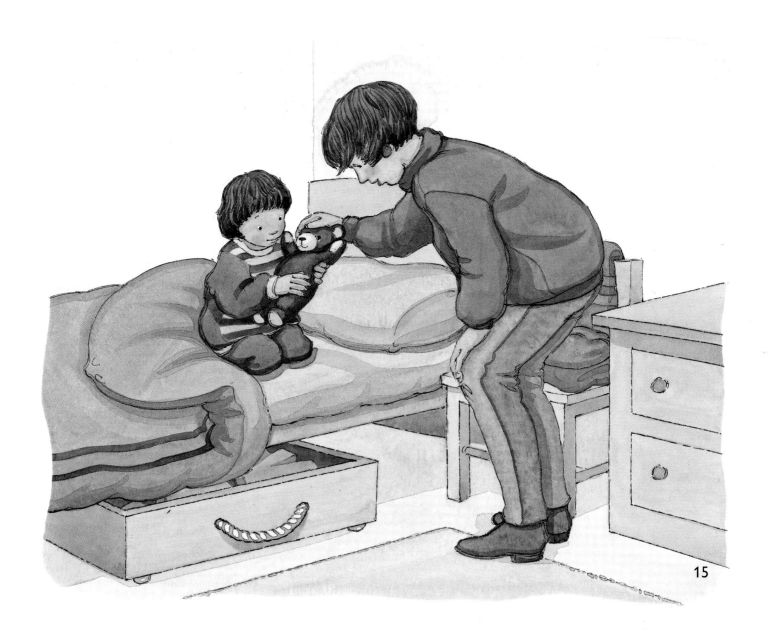

15

Sam and Little Bear

went to sleep.

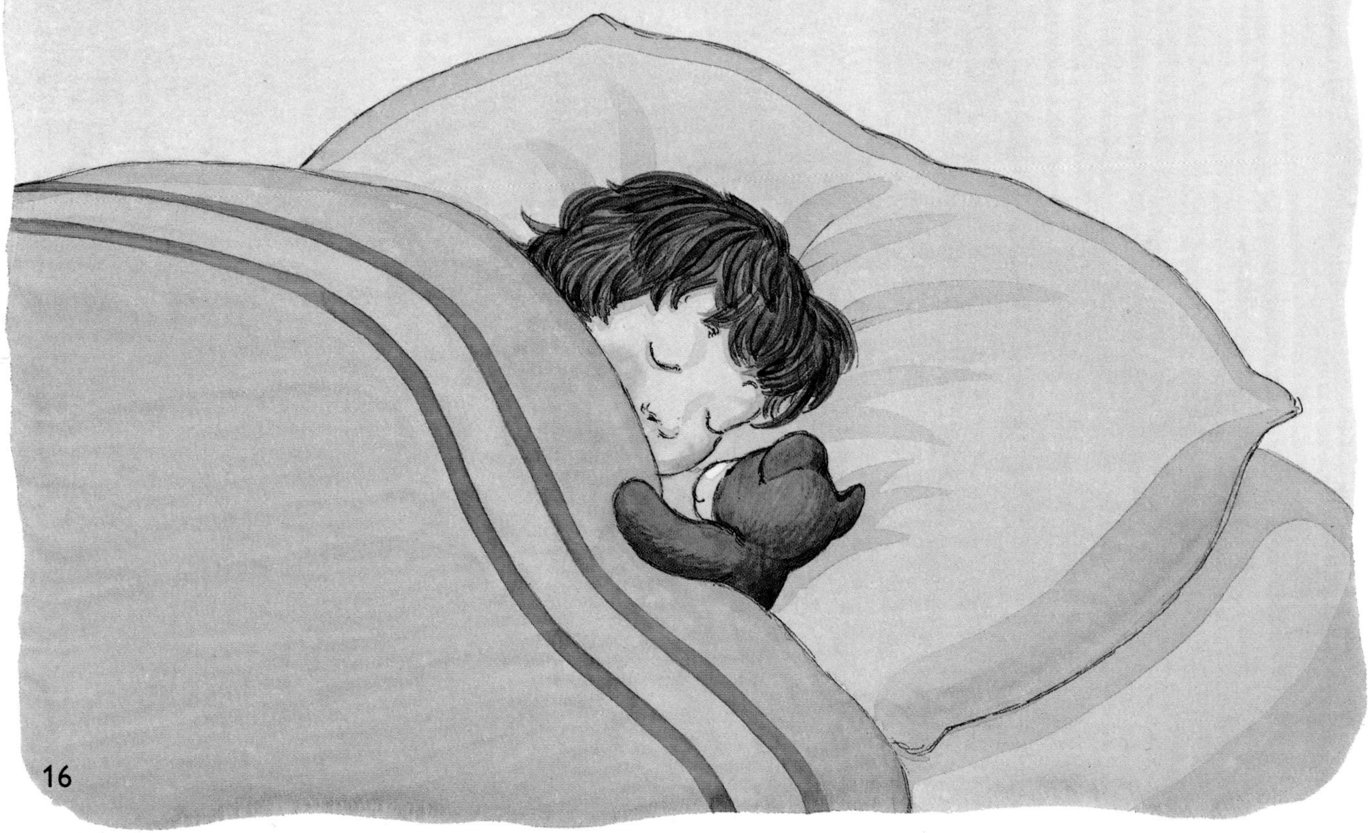